Penguin Education

Papers in Education

G000061078

The Child's Discovery of Space

Jean and Simonne Sauvy

The Child's Discovery of Space

From hopscotch to mazes:
an introduction to intuitive topology

Jean and Simonne Sauvy

Translated by Pam Wells with an
introduction by Bill Brookes

Penguin Education

Penguin Education
A Division of Penguin Books Ltd,
Harmondsworth, Middlesex, England
Penguin Books Inc, 7110 Ambassador Road,
Baltimore, Md 21207, USA
Penguin Books Australia Ltd,
Ringwood, Victoria, Australia
Penguin Books Canada Ltd,
41 Steelcase Road West,
Markham, Ontario, Canada
Penguin Books (N.Z.) Ltd,
182–190 Wairau Road, Auckland 10, New Zealand

First published in France by Editions Casterman, 1972
First published in Great Britain by Penguin Education, 1974
Copyright © Editions Casterman, 1972
This translation copyright © Penguin Education, 1974
Introduction copyright © Bill Brookes, 1974

Made and printed in Great Britain by
C. Nicholls & Company Ltd
Set in Monotype Times

Contents

Introduction to this translation

Children learning mathematics in the early years of school are introduced to numbers as a principal activity. They learn techniques for handling, using and applying numbers which have developed over several hundred years, and the strength of these traditional techniques springs directly from the actual control that they give over the environment.

The basic element in the power of number is uniqueness of succession; given some objects arranged for counting, then, no matter how they are counted, we shall always arrive at the same final number. If this unique correspondence did not exist then we should never have that simplicity of ordering which finally allows us conservation of number.

This seems obvious, yet those of us who have worked closely with young children know the immense variety of ways in which they come to terms with this level of handling of number. To begin to understand the reasons behind this variation, we could look at those experiences thought to be necessary for counting to develop. For instance, what is meant by the phrase 'some objects arranged for counting'? Surely, all objects are arranged for counting in some way or another? In order to decide whether they are indeed arranged or not, we should begin to look at objects and how they appear: battery hens, pigs in sties, cows in fields, ants in a nest. . . . The relationship of place to object seems to be part of the arrangement. We have to be aware of certain kinds of connections before we can be certain about counting.

A six year old out in the country for a picnic went off to count the cars. He did this very quickly. He was then asked to count the people, but declined, saying that 'they wouldn't be in the same place'. When asked what he meant, he replied, 'Suppose someone was there and you counted him and then he went away and someone else came there, you wouldn't count him.' The six year old's ability to differentiate countable objects and noncountable objects is connected with his perception of the relationships between the parts of space to which his attention has been drawn.

The power and simplicity of counting sometimes makes us over eager to see it as an achievement. It seems so obvious and we therefore tend to judge its achievement by certain characteristics. When young children recite the number names 1, 2, 3, 4, . . . , in their correct order and an index finger moves at the right moment for each sound uttered, we can recognize a kind of control. Unfortunately, if at the same time the child's finger does not correspond with the row of buttons that we have put out for him, we often react by saying 'He can't really count yet.' With this state of development, there is no doubt that the child recognizes for himself some characteristic of the uniqueness of counting even though he cannot, at least in the instances the teacher sees, apply it to objects outside himself.

During the period when children are learning to count, they experience the world in a wide variety of ways. Some of these ways are relevant to counting, some are not. Which are important? To whom? To a child conscious of the complexity of making patterns, counting the arrangements may be irrelevant. If counting only appears to him as one of the many ways of seeing the world, then he is as likely to choose other patterns as he is to choose the appropriate one. What will make counting patterns important?

Usually we attempt to make the act of measuring, or comparing in some way, a motive for experiencing counting. Who has most? Least? Who is taller, heavier? Who has most pocket money? We use the possession of property, buying and selling to develop a strong motivation to count. This is not surprising in our society and it should not be surprising to discover that, where a society has no property, there is no counting either! A close study of such societies, for example some aborigine tribes in Australia and certain tribes in Africa, reveals this fact. Yet these societies survive and hence must in some way exercise a control over their own interrelationships and their physical environment.

It is clear that skills in handling numbers are important for us, but our society is growing more complex and there are signs that, in the drive to handle numbers efficiently, we are excluding methods of control which we sorely need to deal with this increasing complexity.

The basic characteristic of number is that of unique succession. With an increasing number of situations where the connections that we have to make are neither unique nor simply ordered, we must look out for other means. It is no longer possible for a person to avoid being involved with other people in a large number of different ways. These ways differ in quality and our ability to survive will, in the end, depend on how skilful we are in dealing with relationships at a large number of differing levels. The child's world is no longer a simple immediate world as, for instance, he can now have the experience of an active TV screen from a very early age.

Just as our ability to count can eventually lead to highly skilled methods of control, so it can be argued that increasingly more insight will be needed into the quality of the connections that can be made in the world in order to survive.

Jean and Simonne Sauvy are deeply concerned with these developments and with how children grow and learn. Their work is based on the Decroly School, near Paris. This experimental school was established after the War and is a place where teachers have cooperated in developing methods of work appropriate to children today. In this book the Sauvys offer one explanation of elementary topological ideas, involving simple notions of connection, neighbourhood and consequential developments. In following children as they explore space, we can see the world in which they learn to count, to connect objects and to distinguish different ways of connection.

But throughout, the aim of this book is to encourage people to think of space in new ways. In everyday life the word 'space' seems to be used for two quite different ideas. When people are asked what they mean by space, they usually answer in terms of vastness, space travel, extending out from the Earth's surface, wide open vistas. . . . This is a natural response and the reader will feel some sympathy for the notion of space as large and empty. There is another use of 'space' which is rarely mentioned, probably because it is a much more prosaic use of the word. Its use is illustrated by such phrases as 'Make a space for me', 'Is there any space?' 'Watch this space', 'Space out the plants!', 'Check that there is enough space', 'Make some more space', and so on. This is a very different use of the word and we usually associate some activity or other with each of the phrases.

It is not surprising that, when asked 'What do you think space is?', people answer with the more intangible notion of vastness, because they are being asked for a description and offer the most general description of space that they can think of. It is not immediately obvious how to describe the space or spaces that are referred to in the second sense, for, each time it is used, it will be linked with the associated activity – gardening, sitting around, car parking, advertising, organizing meetings and so on.

The differences between the two meanings have been stressed, but what, by contrast, do they have in common? Both are associated with emptiness, but this creates problems as it is one of those 'something-for-nothing' words. The other day someone remarked on a trivial incident by saying 'He threw an empty bag of nuts at me'. At first sight it seems that the slightly ridiculous note struck by this sentence should be changed. But, if one suggests 'He threw a bag at me', this would not be an adequate description. What about 'a paper bag'? Even here there would still be a temptation to ask 'Was there anything in it?'. So we retreat to saying 'He threw an empty paper bag at me'. Now it is unclear what kind of paper bag so 'He threw at me a bag which usually holds nuts, but which in this case was empty.' I think in the end I prefer the obvious ambiguity of an 'empty bag of nuts'.

All the phrases used earlier to describe space come from specific situations involving quite specific actions. Their use points to our defining a space for each action. The action itself will define the space. The car park is a simply defined and limited space in terms of cars being parked. If it was used for a game of football when not being used as a car park, then it would be a different space.

We can continue to think of actions defining space and this can be very helpful, but our idea of space has become distorted as we have learnt to measure. By this I mean that we can now think of lengths, areas and volumes and this gives us a definite idea of space being identified by measurements. This is usually done for a practical purpose, but we have become so used to knowing about measurements that we think this is what space is about.

This seems to be a third way of thinking about space which, in reality, is the consequence of generalizing a particular form of the second, concerned with a framework in which things can be done. The making of this framework in terms of common measures developed from the times when such activities, which now rely on common measures, demanded their own frameworks. It is difficult, for instance, to ask now whether the idea of length (as number) came before or after the invention of the measuring ruler. Measuring appears to be a way of dealing practically with many different situations, but there are still far more activities undertaken which do not rely on formal measurement than those that do.

This book deals with matters that reveal themselves more by investigation and thinking than by learning some simple technical skills such as handling a ruler; but the techniques, as a consequence of what is introduced, are not acquired immediately. Here we are more concerned with that aspect of space concerned with movement and possibly having some rules for moving. For example, in a game of chess, the 'moves' of the pieces and the pawns give a framework to the game describing what can happen and making the game possible. The agreement between two people to play is an agreement that exists for the duration of the game in the space governed by the rules. It is easy to see that all formal games are like this and perhaps the idea can be extended to less formally defined activities, which individually show constraints that both define and allow. Writing is such an activity where, in one sense, a piece of paper provides the space, the living room, for the writer, but in a more complex way the writer is held by his skill and in this 'agreement' he demonstrates the space of the skill of writing. Also in a very rich sense we both exist in space and make space. The actor who moves on the stage in such a way as to engage the audience in imaginative responses, making the scene fuller and more vivid, is adding to the simple notion of the measured space of the physical stage. In a simple way and dealing with simple situations, this book begins to show how connections are made and what lies behind the idea of continuity and connectivity.

In the end, the word 'space' has always implied some action that is possible. In the present-day world the possibilities for actions are so diverse and of such different kinds that we have to realize that no one definition will do for 'space'.

In mathematics, which is man's imaginative response to the complexity of the relationships he perceives, there is talk of 'defining spaces' and when we look at this action it is clear that it is a formal action akin to the agreement in a game. For instance, the surface of a sphere can be defined as a two-dimensional surface and for a long time we have used two numbers for latitude and longitude to describe the Earth's surface. This means that ordinary meanings have to change – 'distance' is defined differently as are 'parallel' or 'direction'. We have thus defined a new space for convenient handling of activity on the surface of a sphere. We have to take care how such a space compares with our immediate feelings of flat space – especially when we need a flat map of the sphere!

The authors have used the concept of space partly in an investigation of the way children grow, think and feel. Piaget's observations on the growth of children's concepts of space are sufficiently potent to act as a starting point for us to think afresh about how children, and hence adults, come to exercise the control they do over the space they occupy. One thing is clear, we weren't born with rulers in our hands and yet we move from this lack to a state, some years later, when the ruler in our hand offers one particularly powerful control, amongst many others. During the transition our experience and insight grow; our ability to choose, to manoeuvre and to decide, increases; our particular culture invites us to engage in particular skills rather than others. Eventually we respond in a way which is recognizably within the cultural milieu.

The opportunities for variety have increased and it has become more and more important to look at and think about relationships in and between objects applicable over a wider and wider variety of situations. The growth of topology as a study is a manifestation of this diverse and expansive activity. Once called *analysis situs*, the study of place and position, it is not concerned with measurement but with the more general ideas of connection, closeness, inclusion and neighbourhood.

It is said to be a general and more accessible study, as is shown in the development of this book. A five year old talking at table one day remarked that everything touched everything else. She could describe a simple chain of physical contact and concluded that there was 'a lot of weight' on her. Within this observation is the possibility that children can develop a concept of connection with very powerful consequences.

Topology has, in an elementary sense, been associated with party games, fun at the end of term, a quirky oddity to do with one-sided surfaces, knots and bridges. These are not missing in this book, but here they are embedded in the more serious purposes behind topological thinking of becoming clearer about the general relations of continuity and connection, preparing us for the subsequent specialized study of particular spaces with particular forms in mind. But it is not only in readily definable abstract mathematical objects that one can see the importance of this work. In language, in argument and in relations with people one finds a complexity of interconnections that needs a background of appropriate spatial thinking. One could argue that in the West we have sometimes allowed too linear, too measurable a view of space to prevail, so preventing us from working easily with the complexities that actually face us.

In the future these ideas will develop and become more important as we become better acquainted with the appropriate methods – for instance, the word 'graph' is now coming to mean something more widely applicable than the familiar x- and y-axes at right angles. Someone has recently described a graph as a 'picture with order' and, if such a graph gives extra clarity, then so be it.

Mathematics has long been thought of as the expressed consequence of the perceptions of relationships. As these expressions change, with more and different relationships being expressed in ways accessible to more people, we can expect a growth in the use of these ideas in attempts to illumine the way we think and how we come to think. A most extensive use of topological ideas occurs in Piaget's work on the growth of children's thought. He does not hesitate to use complex ideas, accepting that children growing, acting, thinking and feeling are not particularly simple matters. A sequence of three books concerned respectively with the development of concepts of reality, space and geometry (Piaget, 1954; Piaget and Inhelder, 1956; Piaget, Inhelder and Szemniska, 1960) display a profound attempt to deal with the growth of ways of seeing and controlling the world. In particular, Piaget in his work maintains that children's perception of space intuitively develops from topological space through projective space to Euclidean space. There have been a number of criticisms of Piaget's use of this threefold development and one can be critical of interpretations which suggest that the topological (relational) view of the world simply gives way to the Euclidean (measurement) view of the world. Euclidean space is a sophistication which does not replace topological space, for there is no doubt that measurement space remains topological. Topological properties are more general than the more specific properties of measurement. An interesting interpretation of Piaget's notions could be that these more general properties of neighbourhood and connection are more easily accessible and that they are a necessary acquisition before it is possible to deal with the more precisely defined measurements that Euclidean geometry requires.

The Sauvys have written this book as a contribution to thought about and action with young children in the process of growing into the world. It introduces many of the ideas of topology and, following the text and diagrams carefully, playing some of the games described and carrying out the implied work, will provide a notion of what is changing the face of mathematics. But beyond this the authors are concerned with the need to provide early experiences for children in the light of the new ideas of space that topology has given us. If, in the process of working with children in the ways suggested in this book, quite different observations are made or new revelations of how children think come to light, then the book will have performed the function for which it was written.

Bill Brookes

Authors' preface

All our activities are extended and all our thoughts take place in what modern thinkers call 'space–time'. Although there is a level at which they cannot be dissociated, the concepts of space and of time are sufficiently separate in everyday sensory experience for us to be able to speak of 'space' and 'time'.

The mastery of space is essential for man. In general, it is achieved without too much trouble, but occasionally difficulties arise. This happens, for example, when we emerge from an Underground exit into an unfamiliar part of the city or when we have to interpret, say, the information on a road sign telling us how a motorway interchange works, or the plan showing us how to get to one particular stand in an exhibition on several floors. At such times we may detect a certain inflexibility in our faculties of perception and interpretation, as though they had not received enough training to be able to solve the problems set.

Before we could achieve any sort of mastery of space and build it up into a familiar framework, it was necessary for us as children to discover step-by-step its relational properties. This discovery, as developmental psychology shows, is by no means instantaneous, beginning with the first coordinated movement of the young baby and ending, in principle, at adolescence. We say 'in principle' because, as has just been indicated, the adult sometimes encounters difficulties of a spatial kind.

It seems likely that these difficulties can be attributed to gaps in the education received during childhood and pre-adolescence, for traditional education is concerned only marginally with helping children to 'construct their space'. When it does so, through the medium of geometry, it is almost always confined to Euclidean space, that is, the space of distances and measures which is only one of the three aspects of 'total space' – the topological, the projective and the Euclidean.

Without anticipating the body of the book let us make clear, for those readers who are only imperfectly familiar with mathematical language, (in the elementary sense of the term) that we describe as *topological* relationships in space which involve the concepts of continuity and discontinuity, neighbourhood, region and boundary, open and closed, interior and exterior, disjoint and connected, with and without holes, etc.

The studies of several psychologists – and in particular those by Professor Jean Piaget of Geneva – have shown that these *topological* relationships are grasped by children even before *projective* relationships (left and right, in front and behind, etc.), let alone *Euclidean* ones.

If the educational system shows little interest in topological relationships, this is no doubt due to the assumption that the roots of these relationships are sufficiently well acquired by children in the course of their everyday activities and games so that these provide the young children with numerous opportunities of familiarizing themselves with topological experiences. Through observation they learn very early on that a room is bounded by walls and that these may have openings through which the people surrounding them come and go. Later they learn to distinguish objects according to the kinds of outlines they possess – a banana, because it is 'open', cannot be confused with a bracelet, which is 'closed'. Later still, when they can walk about independently, they practise following lines, jumping across boundaries, or moving a pebble from one square to another in a game of hopscotch.

However, these acquisitions are made in a more or less haphazard way, depending on whether or not a favourable opportunity arises. Accordingly, the gaps are numerous and distinctions, some of which may be essential, are not always made: for example, the difference between an object with a hole in it (through which a string can be passed) and an object which is hollow. The links needed to unite neighbouring concepts are not always forged, and the work of integration and arrangement, characterizing all knowledge which has been truly assimilated, is not always carried out by children in the midst of their spontaneous activities.

Children could learn more easily, and better results could be obtained, if those in charge of their education and, in the first instance, parents, were to enlarge the range of situations relating to topology, to vary their scale and to temper their difficulties.

This intervention presents few problems for two essential reasons:

1 An introduction to topological space does not require reference to straight lines or to measurement and is therefore accessible to children at a very early stage.

2 Learning situations – as the reader will discover from the pages which follow – can very often take the form of games or attractive exercises which the adult has no trouble in presenting.

From this, an educational trend has developed in recent years, particularly in some primary schools in England, America, Canada and France.

If this trend has only become apparent rather belatedly, it is probably for historical reasons, for the essentials of topology, as a systematically studied branch of mathematics, were not developed until the nineteenth century, whereas Euclidean geometry had been developed quite thoroughly by the Greek mathematicians long before our own time.

In addition, the psychological studies by the Geneva school, who were the first to demonstrate the importance of the acquisition of topological concepts in the development of intelligence and their precedence in time over projective and Euclidean concepts, are relatively recent – 1948 saw the first publication of the Geneva school (Piaget, Inhelder and Szeminska, 1960).

Finally, even though the current interest in topology is almost entirely the result of the dual evolution of mathematical and psychological knowledge to which we have just referred, it has received an additional impetus from the pressing demands of our own times, in which complex systems are becoming more and more widespread. In order to make these systems intelligible, there is an increasing tendency to translate them into charts, diagrams and graphs, from the road signs for motorway inter-changes mentioned above through computer wiring diagrams to flow charts for business projects. These graphical representations are of a spatio-logical kind because they translate logical re-lations into a spatial form.

We have said enough to see the importance, both for our-selves and for our children, of anything which allows us to deepen our intuitive understanding of space. With this in mind the present work has been conceived with the dual purpose of extending the information available to adults who wish to keep up to date and to teachers who would like to provide a well-balanced education for the children in their care.

It draws to a large extent on the as yet unpublished experiments which have been continuing for several years at the experimental school of Saint-Mandé (École Decroly) and for a year it has served as the teaching basis for a 'workshop' involving twenty or so parents and schoolteachers.

We have tried – except in the very short final chapter – to steer clear of the kind of abstract mathematics which is the province of specialists, so that we could write our book on a level which is accessible to people with no mathematical back-ground. If we have achieved our goal, it is because the concepts put forward are all borrowed from sensory experience and are close to our familiar world.

We should add that it has been our constant concern to point out the links between concepts at the most basic psychological level and to provide plenty of exercises and games in which these concepts are put to work and demonstrated. Because of this, the substance of our exposition has been somewhat increased, but the experiments which we have carried out lead us to believe that, as a result, the reader's task is greatly simplified.

Chapter 1
Topology and the development of the child's intelligence

Human development takes place in space and in time. Young children become interested in space very early so that, by the second or third month of life, babies coordinate vision and prehension and investigate parts of space both visually and tactually.

As soon as children can walk, they investigate their surroundings even more actively through physical explorations; they learn to distinguish things which are near from those which are far away and so on. They define the external outline of objects by means of touch and sight and begin to differentiate between things which are large, things which are small and things which are medium-sized.

In short, in the course of the first two years of existence, a child 'constructs' what Piaget calls sensory-motor space, by which we mean not the abstract representation of space which an adult creates for himself, but rather something bound up with the individual's senses and with his motor activities.

This space is empirically drawn from experience and will provide the basis for the subsequent formation of representational space. This will take several years and will not be completed until the beginning of adolescence, when intelligence attains the hypothetico-deductive level.

After the age of two, children begin to develop a representation of space by transferring to the level of thought the spatial activities which they have experienced. These early representations are merely rough sketches 'subjected to deformations generated by the irreversible and static nature of intuitive or pre-operational thought' (Laurendeau and Pinard, 1968, p. 14).

This characteristic of a rough sketch is shown, for example, in relation to shapes, particularly those which form the outlines of objects with which children are concerned. The shape of an outline depends on the way in which the successive points of the outline are placed in relation to each other. Examples of such placings provided by children's experiences are extremely varied but many are similar, and children grasp some of these similarities fairly quickly. In particular, they realize very soon that some curves join up with themselves whereas others remain open, or that they are dealing with a smooth curve (part of a circle or an ellipse) and not with an irregular one (star-shaped or triangular outline) which presents hollows, points or serrations. By about five or six, they begin to distinguish between a straight line and a curved one.

As far as surfaces and volumes are concerned, young children similarly distinguish closed surfaces (such as the surface of a ball) which enclose something, from open surfaces (the cylindrical wall of a pipe) which delimit a 'hole'.

Boundaries, whether lines or surfaces, which separate objects from one another, are among children's earliest spatial acquisitions and contribute as much to the 'construction' of the images of objects (making it easier to recognize them) as to the construction of an image of space through the setting up of references (being in a room or outside it, on one side of a stream or the other, and so on). On the other hand, young children may not yet be capable of perceiving systematically those relationships which are projective or Euclidean, that is, relationships which involve perspectives, orientations or distances.

In this context, the studies by Piaget, Inhelder and Szeminska (1960), which have been replicated at the University of Montreal by Laurendeau and Pinard (1968), put forward some interesting ideas that we should consider.

Let us first refer to a series of experiments which the latter two authors carried out at Montreal on some seven hundred children of ages ranging from two and a half to twelve years.

The experimental material consisted of twelve sample figures cut out of strong card and presenting the following shapes: a square, a disc with a hole in it, a closed ring, an irregular cross, a triangle, an open ring, a rectangle, a Greek cross, a circle, an open rectangle, a four-pointed star and a disc with two holes. The task was to identify these shapes without seeing them. The child touched each in turn, indicating, on a card on which all the shapes were represented, the one he had just felt (stereognostic recognition).

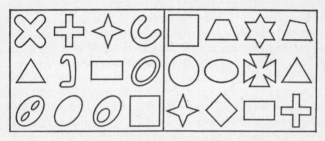

Figure 1   Designs used in the stereognostic recognition test

A subsequent similar test employed twelve figures, some the same as the previous ones and some different. The shapes used were as follows: circle, Maltese cross, square, ellipse, four-pointed star, rectangle, triangle, quadrilateral, Greek cross, trapezium, six-pointed star and diamond.

The responses given by the children were recorded and analysed. It was evident that the younger the children, the greater the number of identification errors that were made, but, more importantly, the errors were not found to be randomly distributed. For example, when feeling the triangle, the young children mistook it more frequently for the star than for the circle; they also mistook the square more frequently for the rectangle than for the open ring and so on.

Statistical analysis of the exact responses made, and of errors regrouped according to category, led the authors to the following conclusions: certain topological relationships are recognized at an early stage, leading children to distinguish filled-in figures from hole-containing figures and open figures from closed figures. Differentiation of straight-edged from curved figures follows soon after but purely metric relationships (dimensions, inclinations, sizes of angles, number of elements, etc.) come last.

Thus we see that, between the ages of four and six, '... the crosses are confused with each other because of their common characteristic of being open figures; likewise confused are the triangle, the square, the rectangle and the other quadrilaterals, on account of their common characteristic of being closed rectilinear figures' (Laurendeau and Pinard, 1968, p. 87).

Another series of experiments carried out by the Geneva team and recently replicated by the researchers at Montreal confirms the developmental primacy of topological relationships over projective and Euclidean relationships.

The task, following the technique employed by Laurendeau and Pinard, was to align eight miniature street lamps on a table between two similarly miniature houses, which could be placed either parallel to one of the sides of the experimental table or at an angle to it. The experimenters recorded not only the configurations obtained at the end of the exercise but also the strategies resorted to by the children.

Commenting on these strategies, they wrote:

Before the age of six or seven, the pre-operational nature of the strategies employed by the child is revealed by the emphasis he places on the topological relationships of simple *neighbourhood* and by the difficulty he experiences in freeing himself from the perceptual implications offered by certain elements of the situation such as the outline of the table upon which he is working. The child, for example, will place the elements (street lamps) next to each other with scrupulous attention to detail, taking care that each base is touching the next one, but without showing any concern for maintaining the same direction, eventually ending up with a meandering curve which is rarely oriented, even when taken as a whole, towards the fixed objective. Another child will only succeed in constructing a straight line provided that he arranges the elements close to the edge . . . (p. 93).

These strategies reveal that the child who is at the pre-operational level relies solely on the relationships of neighbourhood and order.

He proceeds by degrees, making sure that each new element is placed next to the previous one; but he fails to see the necessity for, and furthermore is not capable of, the unification of these successive movements in a way which would enable him to maintain a constant direction and achieve the goal. Given that he can already recognize perceptual straight lines, the child is not unaware of the limitations on his behaviour; but since he cannot represent these straight lines to himself, and therefore cannot anticipate them or mentally reconstruct them, he lacks the internal structures which he would need in order to give direction to his constructions and to resist the suggestion of the perceptual straight lines which are already set up in his visual field (p. 94).

These experiments illustrate the function of 'thinking in pairs' at the ages we have considered. The psychologist Wallon has drawn attention to this process (Wallon, 1945). The pairs of points are seen as pairs merely because of their proximity but the various pairs are considered in isolation, and are not yet integrated into serial chains.

Having summarized the results of several precise experiments carried out on children, we are in a better position to understand the way in which young children construct their mental image of space. It is not a unique image but rather a mosaic of images each one of which is fragmentary, distinct from the others and dependent upon the dominant perceptions provided by experience.

Piaget and his school speak in this context of topological space. The qualification 'topological' is used with reference to mathematics and indicates that, at this level, the only relationships which are regarded as significant are those of a particular kind: neighbourhood or proximity, enclosure (in two dimensions), envelopment (three dimensions), continuity, separation and order. These relationships do not allow us to confer on any given object the status of an object in Euclidean geometry, that is, an object whose points are at invariant distances from each other, nor do they allow us to place an object precisely in a frame of reference.

However, other experiments carried out under the aegis of Piaget and by the Montreal research group, dealing in particular with the way in which children orient themselves and with the distinction they make between left and right, show that, from the age of four or five, projective space and Euclidean space begin to be sketched in against a background of topological space. But the corresponding representations still underline the pre-eminence of the intuitive over the operational and of the egocentric over the global view, as one must expect given the general characteristics of the level of intelligence reached by children of less than six or seven years. For example, a child who is able to distinguish perfectly well between his right and left is incapable of indicating correctly the left and right of some-one facing him. This is because his thought – still at the intuitive stage – centres his attention on 'certain partial and successive aspects of a situation as a whole without being able as yet to devote itself to the activities of integration and compensation necessary to objectivity and to operational reversibility' (Laurendeau and Pinard, 1968, p. 162).

As far as the evaluation of distance is concerned, children of less than six years can in general distinguish near from far but, through lack of ability to measure distances, are obliged to limit themselves to approximate comparisons.

In conclusion, even if, after the age of two to three, children pass from sensory-motor space towards a representational space, the latter is in essence no more than topological; the projective relationships (straight lines and perspective) and Euclidean relationships (metric) are present only in the form of a rough sketch.

Chapter 2
The realm of topology

Let us draw on a plane rubber sheet a closed curve L whose shape is immaterial (Figure 2) and mark five points of which four (A, B, C, D) are on the line and the fifth (X) is not.

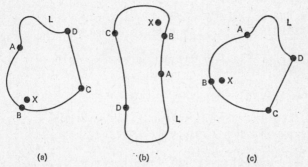

(a)   (b)   (c)

Figure 2

Assume that the points A, B, C, D follow one another on the line in order so that, starting from A and going towards B, the points are encountered in the order B, C, D, while X is inside the curve L and close to B.

With the help of tracing paper, or by some similar method, we can reproduce on a reference sheet of paper the existing configuration which we designate (a).

If the rubber sheet is stretched without folding or tearing it, the curve L is deformed and a new configuration (b) is obtained which we also reproduce on our reference sheet.

Releasing our hold in such a way that the rubber sheet (assumed to be perfectly elastic) returns to its initial tension, the curve deforms and we obtain a third configuration (c).

Let us compare Figure 2a and 2b. In order to make the description clearer, we call the point A in Figure 2b A_b and the corresponding point in Figure 2a A_a. In other words, we are using a suffix notation in which the suffix (in small letters) refers to the figure indicated by the letter.

Comparing our figures, we can make the following observations:

The curve L_b is 'closed' as is the curve L_a;
The points A_b, B_b, C_b, D_b are 'situated on' L_b, just as A_a, B_a, C_a, D_a are 'situated on' L_a;
The point X_b is 'inside' L_b, just as X_a is 'inside' L_a;
The point X_b is 'close to' B_b, just as X_a is 'close to' B_a;
The points A_b, B_b, C_b, D_b are in 'the same order' as A_a, B_a, C_a, D_a;
The number of points marked on L_b is the same as the number of points marked on L_a, four in each case.

Similarly, we may make the following assertions:

The shape of L_b differs from that of L_a. This can be verified by superimposing the tracings and establishing that the two figures cannot be made to coincide;
If we measure with a non-elastic thread the distance separating A_b from B_b and that which separates A_a from B_a, we find that these distances are different;
If we draw a straight line between A_b and B_b and between A_a and B_a we find that these straight lines are not parallel;
If we measure with a protractor the angle $(ABC)_b$, we find that it is not equal to the angle $(ABC)_a$.

On the other hand, comparing Figure 2a and 2c, we find, by superimposing the tracings, that we can make them coincide exactly, A_c covering A_a, X_c covering X_a, and so on.

We may interpret the passage from (a) to (b) and the passage from (b) to (c) as transformations carried out in the plane with each transformation making a point in the original figure correspond to one image point and one only.

The second transformation can be considered as the inverse of the first because the combination of the two transformations allows us to return to the original figure. Thus it follows that to each point in (a) there corresponds a unique point in (b) and vice versa.

Let us designate as T_1 the transformation which enables us to pass from Figure 2a to Figure 2b. T_1 can be characterized by leaving the following properties invariant:

The order of points;
The properties of inside and outside;
The number of points marked on the figure;
The property of proximity.

On the other hand T_1 does not leave invariant either the orientation of the figure or its dimensions. It respects neither parallelism nor the shape of curves and in particular it does not necessarily preserve the straightness of lines – D_aC_a is a straight line whereas D_bC_b is not.

At the end of this first cursory examination we may state the following:

The realm of topology is the realm of those properties of space which remain invariant with respect to bicontinuous deformations typified by those achieved in stretching a rubber sheet without folding or tearing.

Similarly we may state as a first approximation:

Topology is rubber-sheet geometry.

Our reference to a rubber sheet makes it easy to understand the concept of a topological transformation. The mathematician, however, is not content with mental pictures and analogies but requires good, sound definitions.

At this point, it is the bicontinuous transformation which we need to define. However, to do so would require us to introduce the concept of continuity and this cannot be done without recourse to a rigorous definition of the expression 'tends to zero'. We are not equipped, at the elementary level, to become involved in so delicate an exercise so instead we shall concentrate on the intuitive idea.

Roughly speaking we can say that the correspondence $X \leftrightarrow X'$

with $X \in A$ and $X'' \in A'$, where the symbol $\in$ is read as 'belongs to' or 'is an element of', is bicontinuous if, for any given pair p, q in A, there corresponds a pair (p', q') in A' such that whenever p and q approach one another, p' and q do likewise.

Consider two lines, P and Q, which meet at X and define a bicontinuous correspondence between A and its image A (Figure 3).

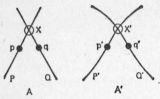

Figure 3

The pair of points p and q can be moved on P and Q respectively and made to meet at X. The images of p and q, p' and q', move upon P' and Q'.

From above, when p and q coincide, p' and q' do likewise. Therefore, the point X, where the lines P and Q meet, corresponds the point X', the point of intersection of P' and Q'.

These brief remarks give some indication of the important position held by the concept of continuity in topological ideas.

As Revuz and Revuz (1966, p. 11) write 'if we were required to give a concise definition of topology, we could say that it is the branch of mathematics which deals with continuity.'

Having briefly defined our area of study, we shall examine in turn each of the various concepts which are an essential part of topology and, wherever possible, we shall suggest ideas for exercises and games which will help children to familiarize themselves with the subject while at the same time taking the opportunity of defining the vocabulary currently in use.

Chapter 3
Exploring the world of topology:
lines and surfaces

Continuity and discontinuity
Ideas

Let us begin with a very simple example. Take a length of thread or string F several centimetres long and place it flat on a table (Figure 4).

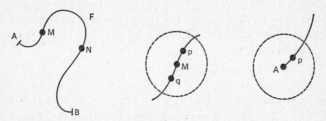

Figure 4

Mark a point M on the thread with a spot of paint. Starting anywhere on the thread, trace a path along it with the point of a pencil in the direction of M. We approach M, arrive in its neighbourhood, and reach it. Continuing slowly on our path, we remain for an instant in its neighbourhood, but on the other side of M and finally we leave it.

This brief exercise shows that M has neighbours on the thread lying on either side of M itself.

For example, in the enlarged portion of Figure 4, p and q are both points in the neighbourhood of M, but they are encountered in the order

pMq or qMp,

where M is 'bracketed' or 'sandwiched' by p and q. The same is true of any point N placed as indicated in Figure 4.

In contrast, the point A occupies a unique position. It has any number of neighbours of (say) category p but none of category q. It is no longer bracketed and marks the limit to our thread (or of the line representing this thread) and is one of the *end points* of F. The same is true of the point B which marks the other end point of F.

Is the special character of the points A and B of a topological nature?

Most certainly, the answer is yes. In order to test this, we have only to consider the effect of a bicontinuous transformation. To do this, we simply arrange the thread differently, for example, by winding it back upon itself (Figure 5a) and considering the new configuration F' as a transformation of F. F' possesses the two unique points, A' and B', and it is clear that A corresponds to A' and B to B'.

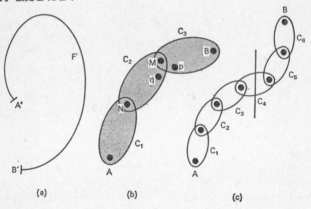

Figure 5

Let us try to clarify the concept of double neighbourhood which we were discussing in relation to the points M and N. To do this, we replace the piece of thread F by a chain made up of solid links C_1, C_2, C_3 (Figure 5b) pivoted together and consider as neighbours all points on the same link.

The point M is at the junction of the two links C_2 and C_3.

By virtue of its being a point in C_3 it has neighbours of category p and, since it is also in C_2, it has neighbours of category q.

On the other hand, point A is in a unique position having neighbours on one link only, that is, on one side only.

The chain AB in Figure 5b, as well as the thread AB in Figure 4, appears to form a whole delimited by extremities. Between these extremities, the constituent points can be considered as overlapping neighbourhoods which ensure an absolute continuity, which is conserved when we deform either the chain or the thread without breaking it.

As an example of continuity, let us consider three separate threads F_1, F_2, F_3 which we tangle together. They lose none of their own identity in the process and once the tangle is unravelled we retrieve the three threads each with its individual characteristics.

Thus the concept of the continuous has been made a little clearer. In order to examine this concept let us start by investigating its converse, using for this a chain AB composed of six elements C_1, C_2, C_3, C_4, C_5, C_6 (Figure 5c). For example, remove link C_4 so that the continuity is 'broken' and C_3 and C_5 become links at extremities. We no longer have a single chain, but two: the chain C_1, C_2, C_3 on the one hand and the chain C_5, C_6 on the other. These chains make up two groups of separated, or discontinuous, links.

For the thread, this is equivalent to supposing that it has been broken by the removal of an intermediate point M, which has given rise to two separate and distinct sections. A discontinuity has been introduced into the initial whole. Whereas previously we were able to follow the thread AB from one end to the other in a single movement without lifting the pencil, this has now become impossible. The overlapping of neighbourhoods has been destroyed instantaneously to leave a discontinuity.

Returning to the chain of Figure 5c, assume that we now remove link C_1. In contrast to our previous finding, we do not obtain two sections nor do we create a discontinuity. Once again the special nature of the extremities is illustrated.

To make the situation even clearer, consider the following

topological transformation. We begin with the 'continuous' line AB, representing the thread AB (Figure 6). Imagine that the

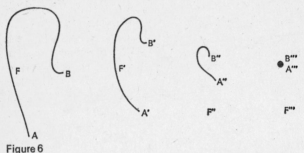

Figure 6

line has been drawn on a highly stretched sheet of rubber. If we allow the sheet to contract slightly, the line F also contracts and is transformed into a line F'. A further contraction gives F'' and finally we can imagine that the contraction is such that the line reduces to a single point, the image of A, as well as B and all the intermediate points.

On the other hand, if we do the same with a discontinuous line which has two distinct sections, the contraction ends in two 'degenerate' lines (each reduced to a single point) which thus remain similarly distinct.

Suggestions for exercises

In Figure 7, two houses, A and B, are joined by various paths, each represented by a single line. Find the continuous path or paths which enable us to travel from A to B and vice versa.

Closed curves

Returning to the chain in Figure 5b, imagine that we bring the two end points together, so that the free end of link A joins up with the free end of link B. The point at which the two ends join now has the same topological status as the intermediate points M and N which we were discussing earlier, since it also has neighbours of the type p and q bracketing it. There are no longer any end points and, wherever we start, we can now travel the whole

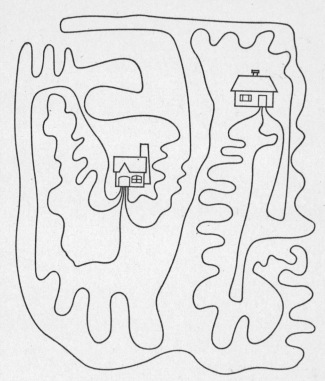

Figure 7 Suppose that all the paths are covered by dominoes or blocks without any discontinuity. If a domino is removed from the centre and placed at the end, then we have a discontinuity

length of the chain without encountering any discontinuities. The line obtained is called a *closed* curve.

We observe immediately that, under the effect of a bicontinuous transformation, every closed curve is transformed into a closed curve and, therefore, we are dealing with a topological characteristic. In order to achieve a closed curve we have only to draw any line which returns to its starting-point. Figure 8 gives some examples.

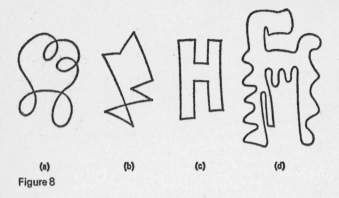

(a)   (b)   (c)   (d)

Figure 8

It may be seen from the figure that several different kinds of closed curve can be drawn. For example, there is a difference between (a) and (c), in the sense that in (c) we do not pass the same place twice whereas in (a) the line crosses itself at certain points.

Therefore (c) appears to be particularly straightforward as far as its topology is concerned. We can subject this curve to a transformation by placing twelve pegs on a peg-board (or twelve drawing-pins on a sheet of plywood) and stretching a length of elastic between them as indicated in Figure 9a. If we now remove the pegs, the elastic takes up its original circular form demonstrating that (a) and (b) are topologically equivalent.

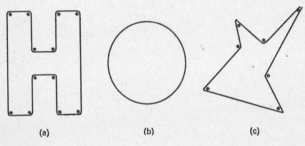

(a)   (b)   (c)

Figure 9

We can thus obtain a class of topologically equivalent figures whose model is the circular curve and to which all polygons such as (c) belong. Any curve belonging to this class is said to be a *simple closed curve*.

Consider the effect of removing any point on a simple closed curve or any link in a closed chain. By so doing a segment AB is obtained, analogous to those which we looked at above in having two extremities A and B between which the curve is continuous. In spite of this cut, we are still able to get from one point to any other on the line without lifting the pencil so that in Figure 10a, we can still trace a path from A to B by following the line L in spite of the cut C. On the other hand, if there are two cuts C and C′, continuity is no longer ensured (Figure 10b). To indicate this discontinuity, we say that the segments CAC′ and C′BC are *disjoint*.

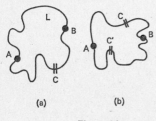

(a)   (b)

Figure 10

Boundaries and regions, interior and exterior
Ideas

Let us draw on a flat surface (plane a) a simple closed curve F, which we can represent by a closed loop of thread that can have any number of meanders but cannot cross itself (Figure 11a).

We know that the line F can be transformed topologically into the circular curve F′ ; point A′ corresponds to point A, point X′ corresponds to point X, and so on.

If A′ and X′ are placed in such a way that they can be considered as the extremities of a segment A′X′ which does not meet F′, the inverse transformation, allowing us to pass from F′ to F,

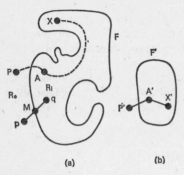

(a)   (b)

Figure 11

makes the segment AX, which likewise does not meet F; correspond to A'X'.

We now displace X' in all possible ways in the plane subject only to the condition that A'X' shall not meet F'. The points X corresponding to X' occupy a certain region in the plane (a) and the segments AX corresponding to A'X' do not meet F. We thus define a group of points X in a which all have the property of being in the same topological situation in relation to the point A. We state that these points define a region of the plane (a domain of points belonging to a certain equivalence class). We can state that, as A is an interior point of F, the set of points X is the interior of F.

Now assume that a point P' is chosen such that any arc A'P' which can be drawn between P' and A' necessarily crosses F'. The corresponding point P in (a) will not belong to the equivalence class previously defined as P will not be situated inside F.

If, in the same way, we search for all the points which behave like P, we define a new equivalence class and thus a new region, which we call the exterior of F. Finally, we must not forget that in the plane (a) there is a set of points situated upon F which belong to neither of these regions.

We have therefore obtained three sets which form a partition of the points in the plane:

1 Set R_i consisting of the points belonging to the interior of F;
2 Set F consisting of the points of F itself;
3 Set R_e consisting of the points belonging to the exterior of F.

Thus we see that a simple closed curve defines, apart from itself, two regions of space, an 'interior' and an 'exterior' which remain invariant under topological transformations.

The regions R_i and R_e have no point in common and are said to be disjoint. The closed curve F forms a division between the two, in the same way that a castle wall creates a division between the interior and the exterior of the castle.

The concept of a boundary can be introduced quite naturally in this context.

Let us examine the topological status of the boundary. Any point M on the boundary line F displays the following special characteristic: it has neighbours in R_i as well as in R_e. This can be verified intuitively by considering an arc pMq which joins a point $p \in R_e$ to a point $q \in R_i$ and allowing p and q to approach M.

Suggestions for exercises and games
Crossing the barriers. For this game we need some coloured counters (red, say) whose underside is clearly marked, for example, with a cross. In addition, we must make a barrier (in the form of a ruler or a line labelled with the same colour as the counters being used) which extends right across the paper. *All* the counters are placed face upwards on the sheet on the same side of the barrier.

The counters can be moved about on the paper but, each time one of them crosses the barrier, it has to be turned over. Passing from A to B, a counter which is face up becomes face down and when passing from B to A a counter which is face down becomes face up (Figure 12a).

The children will soon discover, after a few trials, that all the counters in A will be face up, and all the counters in B face down.

In the same way, on another piece of paper, two enclosed areas are delineated by the barriers P and Q (Figure 12b). Initially all the counters are together inside P and face up. The counters

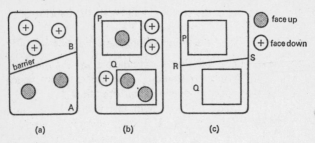

Figure 12

are moved following the same instructions as before so that counters which go into the region Q are all found to lie face up. The game is repeated with a supplementary barrier RS (Figure 12c). What happens in Q?

We can further complicate matters by the introduction of counters of another colour, for example, blue, and an additional barrier which is likewise blue (Figure 13a). The two barriers (or

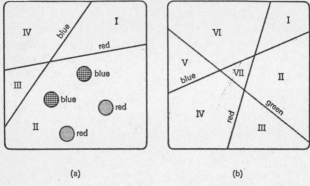

Figure 13

fences) are placed as indicated, and at the beginning all the counters are placed face up in the area marked II.

Again, the counters may be moved on the sheet of paper and each time a counter crosses a fence of the same colour as itself it is turned over, but when it crosses a fence of a different colour it is not.

The children move the counters in accordance with these new instructions. When the four areas are occupied by counters, we find the result:

blue	face up	in II
red	face up	

blue	face up	in I
red	face down	

blue	face down	in III
red	face up	

blue	face down	in IV
red	face down.	

The game can be continued further by adding green counters and a green barrier (Figure 13c). What counters will be found in I, II, III, IV, V, VI and VII if we begin with all the counters face up in II?

The same game can also be played with the fences arranged as indicated in Figures 14a and 14b.

Children who can easily manage this type of problem could be asked to interpret the numerical notations used to label the various regions shown in Figures 15a, 15b, 15c and 15d.

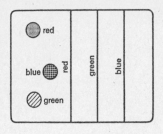

(a)

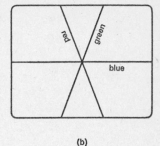

(b)

Figure 14

Note 1. These exercises of a mathematical nature can be linked with exercises in deductive reasoning and in communication

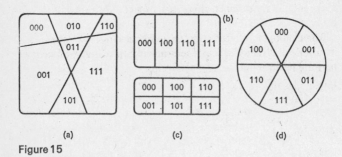

(a)   (c)   (d)

Figure 15

(language practice). The procedure could be as follows; the teacher constructs two identical figures representing, for example, Figure 15a. The lines depicting fences are of different colours or are named accordingly (the 'green fence', etc.) whilst the regions themselves are left unlabelled. One of the boards is given to one team, the second to another team, and each team is also given a 'counter' (small coin, rubber or other object). Team 1 places its counter in one of the regions and attempts to explain to Team 2 which position it has chosen. Team 2 then places its counter in the region which appears to be the one described. When the choice has been made it is checked and comments made on the description given.

Note 2. With nursery-school children, some of the preceding games can be implemented by setting out, in a courtyard or playground, barriers made up of benches, lengths of rope, etc., and allowing the children to represent the counters. The colours are replaced by distinctive marks (such as arm-bands) and, instead of using the alternatives 'face up' and 'face down', we can employ, for example, the alternatives of 'hat on' and 'hat off'. When a child crosses the barrier which bears his distinguishing mark, if he is wearing a hat he takes it off and if he is not wearing one he puts on the one he is holding.

Number of crossings (odd-even). We retain only the red counters and trace on a large sheet of paper a closed polygonal line C such as that represented in Figure 16 with the parallel straight lines indicated by dashes and labelled u, v, w, x. A handful of counters is placed face up inside C and on the lines u, v, w, x. The rules are the same as in the preceding game but the counters may only move along the parallel lines proceeding from left to right.

After a suitable number of moves, we observe that the counters inside C are all face up, and those outside are all face down. The game may be completed by noting the number of crossings made by the various counters for them all to finish at the extreme right-hand side of the area. We observe that all these numbers are odd.

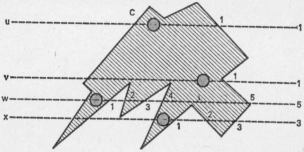

Figure 16

Concept of the 'hole' – connectivity
Ideas

Cut out of a sheet of coloured cardboard a simple closed contour such as L (Figure 17a) and place it on a sheet of white paper. Repeat the operation with a second contour L_1 and cut out a 'hole' following the line L_2 within L_1 (Figure 17b). Let us consider the regions obtained in the two cases (the cross-hatched regions of the figures) and attempt to clarify our intuitive idea of the distinction between the two regions.

We choose two points A and B on the boundary L, joining them by a continuous curve contained within the area and consider this

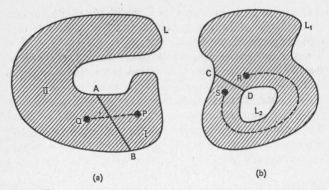

(a)   (b)

Figure 17

curve as a boundary. Whatever the respective positions of A and B, the area under consideration has been divided in two so that, if we cut the cardboard along AB, we obtain two disjoint pieces, destroying the unity of the region.

Moving now to Figure 17b, we see that the boundary CD joining the internal contour to the external contour does not create a new region. If we cut along the curve CD the cardboard remains in one piece and we can still find a path which allows us to go from a point R to a point S without crossing the boundary (for example, the dotted line in Figure 17b).

Thus we have a criterion which enables us to distinguish between the two cases. In addition, it appears that the distinction is a topological one. To confirm this we have only to repeat the exercise using a sheet of rubber.

In order to describe the property possessed by a region of type (a), we say that it is *simply connected*. In all other cases we are dealing with areas which are not simply connected. In other words 'simply connected' as far as surfaces are concerned is synonymous with 'not having holes'.

Exercises

The children are given a game involving pieces of cardboard on which the teacher has drawn a closed contour delineating several regions, some of which are simply connected while others are not (one hole, three holes, etc.). One or more internal boundaries complete each drawing. The exercise consists of enumerating in each case the regions which are inside the contour. To make this enumeration easier, the children can be encouraged to colour the drawing using a different shade for each region.

At the end of the exercise a summary table can be drawn up collectively in which the column headings indicate the number of holes, while row headings indicate the number of boundaries. The corresponding number of regions is written in the relevant square (Figure 18).

Note. If it is thought necessary, this kind of exercise can be introduced to young children by indicating that each large area is an enclosed field containing animals, represented by tokens of different colours. The teacher then says that some of the animals (for example, the red tokens) must be isolated in such a way that they are separated from all the rest by at least one fence (boundary) – how can this be done?

The case of a region which is not simply connected is represented by a field containing one or more ponds each of which is equivalent to a 'hole'.

Order
Ideas and experiments

Tie four knots in a length of elastic and place in each one a scrap of coloured cotton, for example blue (b), yellow (y), red (r) and green (g). Place the elastic on a board covered with a sheet of white paper and trace with a pencil the position of the elastic, marking the position of each of the threads of cotton by a line beside which its colour is noted (Figure 19).

Remove the elastic, placing it in a different position on the paper, stretching it out so as to keep it taut with the help of two drawing-pins A and B. Trace the new position and also that of each of the coloured strands b′, y′, r′ and g′. Remove the elastic and consider the result.

number of holes

	0	1	2	3			
number of internal boundaries 1	2						
2							
3							

no holes
1 internal boundary
how many regions?

2 boundaries
how many regions?

4 boundaries?

1 hole
1 internal boundary
how many regions?

1 hole
2 boundaries

1 hole
3 boundaries

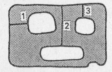

3 holes
3 boundaries
how many regions?

4 boundaries

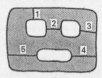

5 boundaries

Figure 18

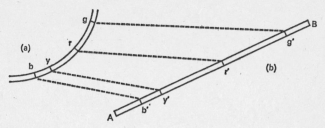

Figure 19

We see that the sequence of colours occurs in the same order on the two drawings: blue, yellow, red, green, and we can now, for example, join b and b', y and y', r and r', g and g' by threads which do not cross one another.

When working with very young children we can put a spot of paint in each position and give one of the tracings to one child and the second to another. Both are then asked to call out loud the colours which they encounter as they work along the elastic starting together from the blue end (or from the green end). After a few attempts, a fair degree of synchronization is achieved and the two voices can be heard saying 'yellow – red – green, almost in unison.

The passage from Figure 19a to 19b can be considered as the product of a bicontinuous transformation. Order, except for the possibility of a complete reversal, is a topological property.

A tin lid, cylindrical or parallelepiped in shape, is stuck to a sheet of card and a string is attached at O where the lid meets the cardboard. On the string, whose other end is free, are markers (perhaps in the form of coloured dots). Initially, the string and the lid are placed as indicated in Figure 20. The position is reproduced on the blackboard or in an exercise book. The string is then wound round the outside rim of the tin and the points a' and b', where a and b meet the rim, are marked. These positions are noted on the initial drawing. Care must be taken that the string is shorter than the perimeter of the lid.

The teacher then marks two points m and n on the line representing the string. The pupils now have to guess, without

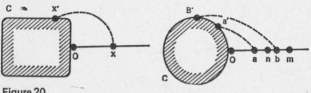

Figure 20

trying it out, roughly where m and n will touch the edge of the lid when the string has been wound round it.

Some related activities
Classification of figures according to topological criteria

Some children are given a series of cards each of which reproduces one of the drawings from Figure 21. They are then asked to sort the cards according to one or more criteria of their choice. There are numerous possible classifications.

Some children will recognize a distinction between lines, e.g. (a), and surfaces, e.g. (g). Concentrating first on the lines, we can group together those which are open (b) separately from those which are closed (r). Similarly, we can distinguish between continuous lines (m) and discontinuous lines (c).

If, on the other hand, we consider the surfaces, a division can be made into two equivalence classes: simple surfaces (n), on the one hand and surfaces with holes (j) on the other. These last can be subdivided into three classes: surfaces with one hole (g), two holes (j) and three holes (i).

Young children will sometimes discover different and quite legitimate classifications ('points', 'rounded edges', 'zig zags').

We can also make use of these exercises to clarify the logical and group concept of 'nested classes' which can be represented by diagrams of the 'chest of drawers' or 'tree' variety (Figure 22).

The numbers in roman numerals demonstrate the one-to-one correspondence between the examples in the drawer and in the tree diagrams.

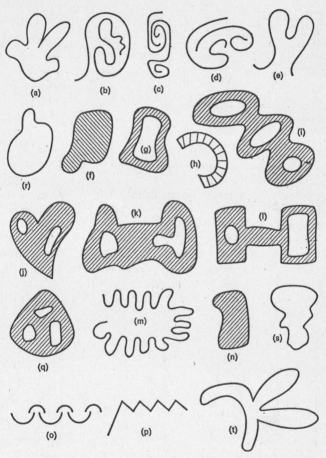

Figure 21

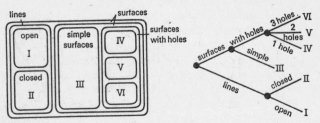

Figure 22

The game of 'Life'

This game was invented by the mathematician John Conway (Gardner, 1970) and is suggested here because it reveals certain topological aspects and allows us to put into practice, in an intellectually stimulating way, some of the concepts which we have come across previously.

The group of squares on a chessboard may be considered as forming a 'mesh of neighbourhoods'. Two squares which have at least one side or one corner in common are considered to be 'neighbours'. For example, the shaded square (Figure 23a) has as its neighbours squares 2, 3, 4, 5, 6, 7, 8 and 9, but not squares 11, 12 or 13.

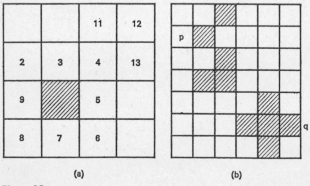

(a)   (b)

Figure 23

We assume that each square can be occupied by an elementary cell of a hypothetical living organism. Several elementary cells are considered as belonging to a single organism whenever they form a continuous chain of neighbours (configurations p or q in Figure 23b). In addition, we assume that individual cells are born, survive or die in accordance with certain rules of evolution.

Development proceeds in a step-by-step fashion and at each stage the birth, survival or death of a cell in any particular square depends on the number of cells occupying neighbouring squares immediately beforehand:

Every cell in a square with two or three neighbouring cells survives for the next generation;
All other previously existing cells die;
In every empty square with exactly three neighbouring cells, a new cell is born.

We can illustrate these rules as follows:

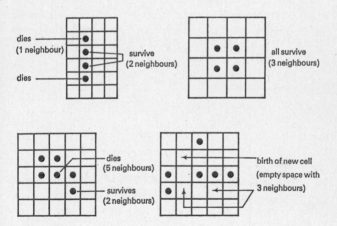

Figure 24

The game requires the setting up of an arbitrary configuration of cells for the initial state (state 1) and applying the above rules in order to arrive at a subsequent state (state 2), and so on through as many 'generations' as possible.

The interest in the game lies in the fact that, although the rules are apparently so simple, they lead to remarkably complex and diverse evolutionary forms: organisms are born and die, while some tend towards a stable or oscillating form (the latter periodically returning to the same state). However, the game requires a great deal of attention precisely because of the complexity of the configurations involved.

In the school curriculum, this game has the merit of demonstrating the importance of the starting configuration on the result obtained by the application of a transformation. We are dealing here with 'state–operator–state–operator' chains which are much less monotonous than those commonly obtained when playing with logic blocks, for example.

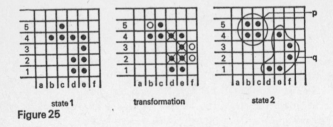

state 1   transformation   state 2

Figure 25

The most convenient way of actually playing the game is to take a sheet of squared paper and proceed as follows (Figure 25). The starting configuration (state 1) is drawn twice, the cells being indicated by black dots. The first diagram is used for reference and the second as a rough draft for when the transformation from one state to the next is carried out. On the latter all the cells are examined to see whether they are to die or survive, a cell which dies being marked with a cross. For example:

(c, 5) three neighbours (black dots): survives
(b, 4) two neighbours: survives
(c, 4) three neighbours: survives

(d, 4) four neighbours: dies
(e, 4) two neighbours: survives
(e, 3) four neighbours: dies
(d, 2) four neighbours: dies
(e, 2) four neighbours: dies
(d, 1) three neighbours: survives
(e, 1) three neighbours: survives.

Next we examine the diagram for births, which will occur in any empty square having exactly three cells in neighbouring squares. This is the case in (b, 5), (f, 3) and (f, 2). A small circle is drawn in each of these squares.

We are now in a position to work out state 2 on a third diagram. We record, as black dots, the cells which have survived and those which have appeared. This new diagram is taken as the starting point for a further transformation.

A comparison of states 1 and 2 shows that our organism has undergone a considerable change from one generation to the next. Indeed, according to our criterion, it has given birth to two distinct organisms (labelled p and q on the diagram). It is possible that on the next 'move' these two organisms will coalesce again into a single form.

The game may also be played on a chessboard with the help of counters, but great care must then be taken to avoid making a mistake since no record exists of the successive states.

Mazes

Mazes are excellent examples of topological figures and can equally well be drawn on a sheet of paper or on a sheet of rubber. As our first example, consider the following exercise.

Study the maze in Figure 26a which has its entrance at A and its exit at B.

1 Find the path which allows you to go from A to B;
2 Trace with the point of a pencil the wall situated on the right of the path you have just followed. Do the same thing with the wall which is on your left as you enter.

From this deduce that someone who had been blindfolded as he entered at A would have found the exit without difficulty.

Figure 26a

A second example of a maze is provided by Figure 26b. Having studied the drawing, answer the following questions:

1 How many simple closed lines does the drawing contain?
2 Can you distinguish an 'interior' and an 'exterior'?
3 Let a thread cross the design from one side to the other without making a loop and indicate, for various positions of the thread, the number of intersections which it makes with the lines of the diagram. What do you observe? Would you have been able to predict this result?

Figure 26b

A third example of a maze is given in Figure 26c. Its structure differs from the previous ones, since it is made up of four curves each having one extremity at O, while the other is free. With schoolchildren this can be set up in practice by using four lengths of coloured thread knotted together at O. A counter is then placed between two of the threads, for example at X.

In which direction must we set off in order to arrive at the exit A by the shortest possible route?

Note. Constructing mazes can give rise to some interesting practical exercises. The children can build them out of clay or plasticine inside the lid of a large cardboard box, for example.

Figure 26c

It should be possible to roll a small ball easily along the paths provided; similarly, it should be possible to place a flexible cord in the channels bordered by modelling clay so that it follows all the meanders of the path leading from the entrance to the exit of the maze. This cord will of course be called 'Ariadne's thread'.

Even if it is thought advisable to provide the children with a model for the design of the first maze which they build, each child can subsequently invent a maze of his own design, thus allowing him to bring his own creative powers into operation.

Chapter 4
Exploring the world of topology: volumes

Three-dimensional space (volumes)

Up to now we have confined our attention to the two-dimensional space represented by the skin of a rubber ball or inner tube, a table top or a sheet of paper. In other words we have been talking about surfaces. The concept of a surface is an intuitive one and we have made no attempt to define it.

In fact, real objects are volumes which always have a thickness; they are sets of 'points' arranged 'in all possible directions' and are embedded in space (qualified as a 'three-dimensional' space).

Our perception is such that when we see and touch objects we encounter only the surfaces which delimit them. This does not, however, prevent us from formulating what is, from the perceptual point of view, the extremely complex concept of volume, to which we shall now devote a brief chapter.

When dealing with volume and three-dimensional space, the rubber sheet is replaced by a ball of modelling clay. Accordingly, let us take a lump of modelling clay and, rolling it in our hands, make it into a ball or sphere.

Starting with the ball we can, without making a hole through it, change its shape to form ellipsoids, cylinders, parallelepipeds and polyhedra, or reproduce as many arbitrary shapes as we wish: potato, banana, and so on. The various solids thus obtained are all topologically equivalent.

On the other hand, our transformation does not allow us to pass from the sphere to a solid having the form of an anchor ring or torus (Figure 27b).

To make the distinction clearer, we draw on the sphere in Figure 27a a simple closed curve C with two points p and q, one on each side of it. This acts as a boundary for points on the surface of the sphere and delineates two regions, one inside the

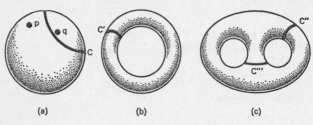

Figure 27

curve C, the other outside. Let us now divide the ball of clay
with a cutting tool using the curve C as a guide. We now no
longer possess a single solid but two distinct solids. The surface
across which the cut was made is a boundary surface between the
two solids.

By contrast, the curve C′ on the torus in Figure 27b does not
delimit two regions on the surface of the torus and, if we cut
through it following C′, we find ourselves still confronted with a
single solid. We thus have a criterion for distinguishing between
topologically distinct solids. Furthermore, we can generalize so
that Figure 27c represents a solid with two holes and we observe
that two cuts can be made in this case – for example following
C″ and C‴ – without destroying the characteristic of topological
unity of the object under consideration (the modelling clay can
be used to help 'visualize' this more easily).

Let us work with some everyday solids. Consider, for example,
a parallelepiped box such as that in Figure 28a.

When we examine its surface by sight or touch, we can
distinguish the faces of which it is composed, for example the
face cdhg which forms the underside of the box or the face abdc
which forms one of its lateral surfaces. Equally apparent are
some conspicuous curves: the simple closed curves (made up of
straight lines) which serve as boundaries for the various faces.

The points of a boundary, unlike the points of a curve such
as C, have neighbours on adjacent faces; for example M has as

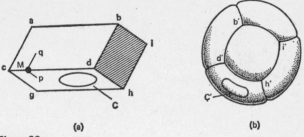

(a)   (b)

Figure 28

neighbours p and q (p ∈ face cdhg, q ∈ face abdc). Among the points on the boundary, some are of particular interest because they are situated at the meeting point of several boundaries. These points are *vertices*. Following current terminology, we shall speak not only of faces and vertices but also of *edges*, each of which is that part of a boundary which joins two adjacent vertices.

Let us now imagine that the faces of our parallelepiped are made of sheets of rubber whose edges have been joined together in pairs, as in the construction of a football. We now perform a topological transformation, providing our 'bladder' with a valve and blowing it up. The faces distort, the edges become curved, the vertices flatten out and we end up with the ball in Figure 28b upon which are found the eight points a′, b′, c′, ..., h′ (the transforms of the points a, b, c, ..., h) and the simple closed curve C′ (the transform of C), etc.

The topological relationships are conserved: a′, b′, c′ and d′ remain in the same order in relation to each other as a, b, c and d; C′ is situated inside the region c′d′g′h′ just as C is situated inside the region cdgh.

A close kinship is thus apparent between the topological problems encountered in relation to surfaces in two-dimensional space and those encountered in relation to volumes in three-dimensional space.

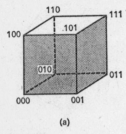 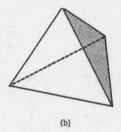

(a)   (b)

Figure 29

Exercises

Neighbours on a cube

Take a box which is cubic or parallelepiped in shape and number its vertices as indicated in Figure 29a. We describe as 'neighbours' of any particular vertex those vertices which are directly linked to the reference vertex. For example, vertex 100 has as neighbours 000, 101 and 110.

Take each of the vertices in turn and draw up a list of its neighbours. Study this list and note any conclusions which might be drawn. Try to find a logical presentation of the results.

Neighbours on a tetrahedron

Repeat the previous exercise using the tetrahedron in Figure 29b. Draw on the surface of a ball, an apple, etc., the set of lines and points corresponding to the set of edges and vertices of the tetrahedron. (If you have difficulty in grasping the above question, imagine what would happen if you were able to 'blow up' the tetrahedron into the shape of a sphere.)

Solids with and without holes

The distinction between solids with and without holes is made by generalizing from the concept that distinguishes those surfaces with holes from those simply connected surfaces without.

Collect together a number of everyday objects, some of which have holes and some of which have not: the cap of a pen, the dispenser for a reel of sellotape, a cork, a glass, a bottle, a funnel, a ring, a necklace, a bracelet, a school cap, a key, a drinking straw, a pair of scissors, a spectacle case, a waste paper basket, both parts of a matchbox (the 'box' and the 'drawer'), etc.

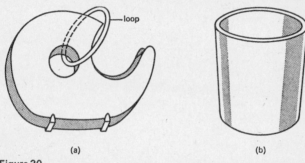

(a)   (b)

Figure 30

We now set about the task of sorting them into two categories: those with holes and those without. For this we can make use of the following criterion: if, with a piece of thread, we can make a closed loop which cannot be removed from the object without being cut, we have a solid with a hole. Otherwise, the solid does not have a hole even if, as in the case of a glass for example, it appears to have one (Figure 30).

Chapter 5
Topological maps and diagrams

We know that the nature of thought is to 'operate' on abstract representations. Throughout the previous chapters we have constantly resorted to representations which, because of the limitations of the printed page, were necessarily plane representations realized in the shape of drawings consisting of points and lines.

From the naïve viewpoint which we adopt in the present work, our topology cannot exist without representative images or illustrations. Conversely, the technique of drawing representative images requires the 'topo-logical' infrastructure provided by the topological concepts which we have been studying up to now.

In the present chapter we propose to develop this aspect of topology, an aspect which seems to be particularly suited to promoting the development of intelligence in children.

Plans, maps and diagrams

Consider an aerial photograph of, say, part of a village with houses, gardens and roads, paying particular attention to the roads (Figure 31a). They are organized in such a way that it is possible to get from any particular house P in the village, to any other house Q. If I wish to explain to a friend who lives at P the

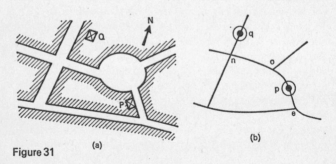

Figure 31

route which he should take in order to visit me at Q, I show him the position of the two places on the photograph and, using a pencil, trace the paths which he can take in order to go from P to Q.

Nevertheless, my friend, not trusting his memory, proposes to transcribe on to a sheet of paper the essential points of information which he will need in order to find the route. He does this with the help of a diagram of the kind in Figure 31b. He records only the essentials, that is, the position of the roads in relation to each other – each road being represented by an arc, and each crossroad by the crossing of two lines – while the positions of the houses are marked by points on the line representing the road on to which the houses face.

Figure 31a is a map of the area (the space represented being projected on to a plane surface) whereas Figure 31b is a diagram of the network of communications.

There is a topological correspondence linking the lines drawn on the map to indicate the paths to be followed and the lines on the diagram representing these paths. Dimensions are not respected (the diagram is not 'to scale'), neither is orientation (the diagram carries no indication regarding the direction of north). Order, on the other hand, is respected, as are the relative positions (of the interior/exterior kind) of lines and points. The diagram thus appears to be a convenient method of reformulating a body of information of a topological nature.

The 'map' of the Underground provides a good example of such a diagram. It indicates both the correct sequence of stations and the points of intersection where interchanges are made.

Let us consider another example, that of a river basin. The map, drawn to scale and oriented (with respect to true north), gives a relatively detailed representation of the course of a river and its tributaries (Figure 32a). The diagram in Figure 32b is topologically equivalent. It is, in a way, a 'structural diagram' which bears only those features which are relevant to its intended use.

We might remark here, without labouring the point since the subject is a vast one, that the representations of figures which

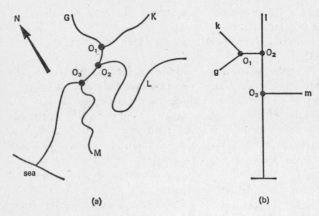

Figure 32

children produce when they begin to draw are themselves related to diagrams. For a child, Figure 33a adequately represents the head of a man because it is topologically equivalent to the set of lines constituting the face that he sees: the outline is closed and so are the outlines of the eyes, each of these two outlines is inside the outline of the face, and they are all disjoint. The outline of the ears is similarly closed and each is placed outside the outline of the face but contiguous with it.

Again, the drawing in Figure 33b represents a man quite adequately since the essential features of the human structure are contained within it.

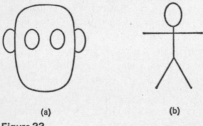

(a)   (b)

Figure 33

Basic diagrams

Amongst the diagrams to which we refer constantly, not only in mathematics but in everyday life, there are some which recur continually, either individually or as parts of more complex schemas. Let us review some of these basic diagrams.

We can begin with binary branching (Figure 34a) which is the topological representation of an alternative. At a branching (or node), a path *bifurcates*, dividing into two. Branchings can be assembled in sequence, and thus we obtain a binary tree (Figure

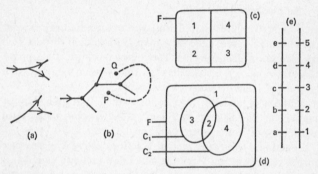

Figure 34

34b). The characteristic feature of a tree is that it does not contain any closed lines. The space around a tree is connected: a path can always be found which goes from P to Q avoiding the branches of the tree.

The next basic diagram is a cross associated with a simple closed boundary (Figure 34c). The cross marks out four regions inside the simply connected area surrounded by a boundary F. To go from one region to another, we must pass over at least one branch of the cross, on the assumption that at the point of intersection both branches are considered to be present. This is the Carroll diagram.

The Euler–Venn diagram (Figure 34d) has some properties in common with the preceding one: the two circles C_1 and C_2 also divide the area inside F into four regions.

A useful exercise for children who are beginning to use diagrams such as these is for them to discover their common structure by setting up a one-to-one correspondence between the regions of (c) and those of (d) by placing different coloured counters two at a time in each of the regions of (c) and (d). The scale is represented by distinct marks inscribed along a line (Figure 34e) with the order generally indicated by reference to the order of the natural numbers (1, 2, 3, . . .) or to alphabetical order (a, b, c, . . .).

Planar topological graphs

Returning to Figure 31a, which allowed us to reproduce in essence the information presented on a map, we note that this diagram is made up of line segments. These lines meet at certain points to form nodes or intersections so that we can mark a point situated on a line and indicate its position by reference to the two special points (nodes or intersections) which bracket it. For example, on the diagram in Figure 31b the point p is situated between o and e or, in other words, on the arc oe.

In addition this figure can be described as *arcwise connected* in the sense that, by following successive arcs, we can always traverse the diagram from any point situated on one line to any point situated on another line: it is a continuous figure.

We shall now systematically examine this class of diagrams.

Terminology

Each 'special point' of a figure, that is, each point where lines meet or which constitutes an extremity of a line, is called a *vertex*. On Figure 35a the vertices are identified by the capital letters A to G.

Each line which joins two adjacent vertices is called an *edge* or an *arc*. For example, r is an arc joining the adjacent vertices A and B. However DG is not an arc since between D and G there is a vertex E. In the case where the second vertex is identical with the first (the 'pair' GG in the figure) the arc is called a *loop*. On the diagram there is one single loop: the closed circuit Bp Cq B does not constitute a loop because the vertex C inter-

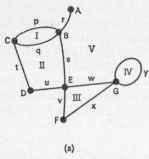

(a)

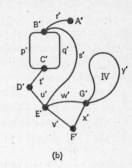

(b)

Figure 35

venes. On the diagram the edges are marked by lower-case letters from p to y.

We note that there may be several arcs or edges between the same pair of vertices. This is the case for p and q which both join B to C (or C to B).

In the example we have chosen, consecutive vertices are considered in any order: A B or B A, for example. We are thus considering pairs of consecutive vertices and not ordered pairs. If it were otherwise, the figure would be directed and the oriented path A B, for example, would have to be distinguished from the path B A.

Next we consider the parts of space delimited by the lines of the figure. These segments of space are known as *regions*, *faces* or *areas*. In Figure 35a the regions are labelled by the numerals I to V. Region V is outside all the lines of the figure and is frequently overlooked, particularly when using the term 'face' since this term is commonly associated with an enclosed part of space. It is, however, essential that we consider it as a region, because it corresponds to the general definition: any two of its points can be joined by a simple arc without crossing any edges.

Finally, following current terminology we call the figure under consideration a *planar topological graph*.

In this expression, the word *graph* is taken in the sense of 'graphical representation'; the word *planar* signifies that the representation lies in the plane; and the term *topological* signifies that we are interested in topological properties alone to the exclusion of the orientation, shape and dimensions of the figure.

Thus we could equally well use both Figures 35a and 35b for the problems we are considering here. They are topologically equivalent, being two distinct representations of the same graph.

In the subsequent exercises we shall occasionally refer to the number of edges which leave (or arrive at) a single vertex: we shall call this number the *degree* of the vertex. By convention, when we have a loop at vertex A, the two extremities of the arc formed by the loop are counted separately so that the degree of A is two for a single loop. On the graphs in Figure 35a we have:

vertex A	degree one
vertices D and F	degree two
vertex C	degree three
vertices B, E and G	degree four.

Exercises

The following exercises, puzzles and games may help us to:

Transfer the information given by a map on to a planar topological graph;
Make practical use of such a graph;
Recognize equivalent graphs.

First of all, an exercise concerning itinerary and order. The map shown in Figure 36 represents part of a town with a school. Every morning the school bus leaves the garage in St John's Road. It has to pass in succession various points in the town, where the children are waiting to be driven to school. The children are, in alphabetical order:

Carol, John, Mary, Paul and Peter.

The driver's instructions are that he must only go down each road once. Consider the following problems:

1 Write down the list of roads which you would go down in turn if you were the bus driver. Are there several, one or no itineraries which satisfy the required condition?

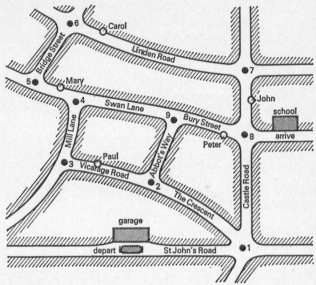

Figure 36

2 Give the name of the child who is the first to get into the bus and the name of the child who is last.

3 Draw up the corresponding planar topological graph taking the numbered crossroads to be its vertices and the roads its edges (Figure 37). The problem is essentially that of getting from vertex 1 to vertex 8 while being obliged to pass via the edges (2, 3), (4, 5), (6, 7), (8, 9), (7, 8).

4 Make the problem more complicated by placing additional children on edges (1, 2), (3, 4), (5, 6), (4, 9), (7, 8), (1, 8). Can the bus still collect the children without taking the same road twice?

Here is another exercise known as the problem of the Caliph of Baghdad. A certain Caliph of Baghdad, wishing to test the

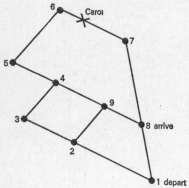

Figure 37

intelligence of those who sought the hand of his daughter, caused them to be set the following problem.

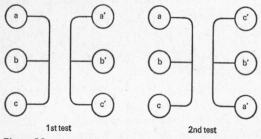

1st test   2nd test

Figure 38

In Figure 38 each vertex, such as a, has to be joined with a continuous line to the corresponding vertex a′ in such a way that the lines drawn do not meet any other line. As may be seen, the solution is quite simple for the first diagram. In the second case, however, there is no solution, as can be verified for two individual cases with the help of the diagrams in Figure 39. In the two cases shown, c is *inside* and c′ is *outside* the shaded area.

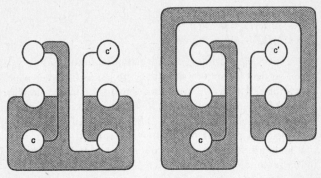

Figure 39

A third exercise puts forward a method of 'storing' information contained in a planar topological graph by means of *Boolean variables* (variables with two values). Consider the planar graph

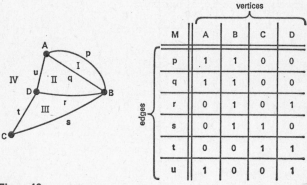

Figure 40

M	A	B	C	D
p	1	1	0	0
q	1	1	0	0
r	0	1	0	1
s	0	1	1	0
t	0	0	1	1
u	1	0	0	1

represented in Figure 40, which has the following characteristics (we use the letters V, E and F to denote the number of vertices, edges and faces respectively):

Vertices: A, B, C, D   so V = 4,
Edges: p, q, r, s, t, u   so E = 6,
Faces: I, II, III, IV   so F = 4.

The graph carries a store of information telling us, for example, which vertices (taken two at a time) are joined by which edges. This information can be stored in another form using a Boolean matrix M set out as indicated in the table. This matrix is read as follows: p is joined to A and to B but not joined to C or to D; r is joined to B and to D, but not to A or C; and so on.

Adding up the 'ones' in the columns we obtain the degree of the corresponding vertex:
degree A = 3,   degree B = 4, ...

The fourth exercise is the converse of the preceding one. Given a Boolean matrix (Figure 41), we have to find a corresponding planar graph. One possible representation is shown (remember

	A	B	C	D	E
p	1	1	0	0	0
q	0	1	1	0	0
r	0	0	1	1	0
s	1	0	0	1	0
t	1	0	0	0	1
u	0	1	0	0	1
v	0	0	1	0	1
w	0	0	0	1	1

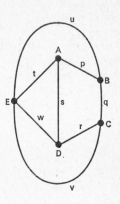

Figure 41

that in order for the graph to be planar no edge should meet any other at a point other than a vertex). The route A B C D A E B, marked with arrows on the matrix, can be traversed with a single stroke of a pencil.

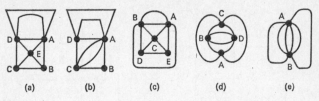

Figure 42

The last exercise consists in identifying among a series of planar topological graphs (Figure 42 a, b, c, d, e) those which are equivalent (the vertices are marked by capital letters; a change of direction does not constitute a vertex).

Hopscotch. Here we remind the reader of the game of hopscotch which children have played since time immemorial and which can be considered as a game with a topological basis.

There exist numerous variations, but the principle is always the same: a group of regions is drawn on the ground and the player has to throw a pebble into each one in turn, rejoin it by 'hopping' without touching the boundaries of the areas, pick up the pebble and return, still hopping, to the starting-point. Numbers written within the areas prescribe the order in which these must be tackled. In no case must the pebble or the player's foot rest on a boundary. If the rule is broken, the whole turn must be taken again. The game is won by the first player to complete the sequence. Figure 43a represents a frequently occurring layout but there also exist more complicated versions.

The game of sprouts. This game, invented by Conway and Paterson (Gardner, 1967), is for two players, the winner being the player who succeeds in blocking his opponent.

Three (or more) points A, B and C, are drawn on a sheet of paper. These will become the vertices of a planar topological graph. Each player in turn draws an arc ('sprout') joining two vertices and adds a vertex anywhere on this arc, exploiting two vertices to create one new one. The game would continue indefinitely but for the additional rule: the degree of each vertex is

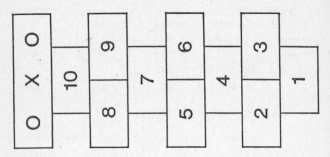

Figure 43

limited to three (not more than three arcs may arrive at the same vertex). At some point the graph reaches saturation. The first player unable to draw a new arc is the loser.

In Figure 44, by way of example, we have drawn the succession of graphs corresponding to the early stages of the game and then the final graph (when further play becomes impossible).

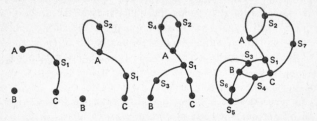

Figure 44

Euler's formula

The mathematician Euler (1707–83), a forerunner of modern topology, studied the relationships that are found between the number of faces, edges and vertices of polyhedra, and discovered in this context a formula which is remarkable in its simplicity. It will be discussed later, but we shall present here the equivalent of his result as an example in planar-graph theory.

Consider some planar topological graphs of increasing complexity. In each case we can record the values of:

V, the number of vertices,

E, the number of edges,

F, the number of faces.

We start with the simple case of two vertices with V = 2 (Figure 45).

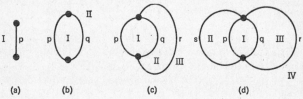

(a)   (b)   (c)   (d)

Figure 45

From this:

E = 1, F = 1   for (a),

E = 2, F = 2   for (b),

E = 3, F = 3   for (c),

E = 4, F = 4   for (d).

Each time we create an edge, we automatically create a new region. Consequently, in the case where V = 2, we will always have the equality E = F.

What about an even simpler case in which there is one single vertex and one or more loops? Let us examine this new situation, for which V = 1 (Figure 46):

E = 0, F = 1   for (a),

E = 1, F = 2   for (b),

E = 2, F = 3   for (c),

E = 3, F = 4   for (d).

We see that in the case where V = 1, we have the relation,

E = F − 1,

that is, the number of edges is one less than the number of faces.

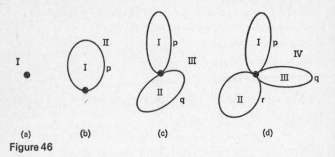

Figure 46

Let us return to the case of two vertices (V = 2) but with some loops introduced into the diagram (Figure 47):

E = 2, F = 2 for (a),

E = 3, F = 3 for (b),

E = 4, F = 4 for (c).

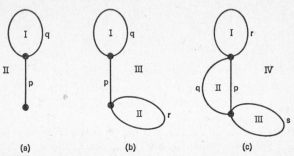

Figure 47

We observe that the equality found previously, E = F, is confirmed once more and this formula is general for the case where V = 2.

Let us consider a graph with three vertices, V = 3 (Figure 48):

E = 3, F = 2 for (a),

E = 4, F = 3 for (b) and (c),

E = 5, F = 4 for (d).

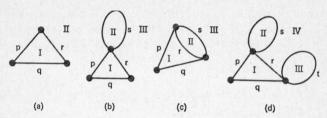

Figure 48

With $V = 3$, the number of edges is greater by one than the number of faces, $E = F + 1$.

Let us now look at some more complicated graphs (Figure 49).

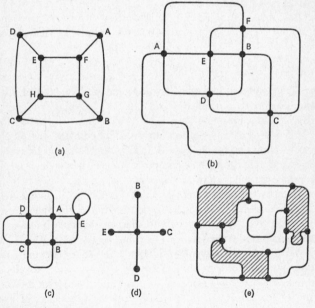

Figure 49

Draw up a table and enter the results obtained from counting
the vertices, edges and faces for the four cases (a), (b), (c) and
(d) (Figure 50). Careful study of this table allows us to demon-

graph	V	E	F
(a)	8	12	6
(b)	6	12	8
(c)	5	10	7
(d)	5	4	1

Figure 50

strate a relationship between F, V and E, which is confirmed in
the four very dissimilar cases we have examined. This is the
relationship,

$$E = F + V - 2,$$

which we may express as: 'For the figures we have studied, the
number of edges is smaller by two than the total number of faces
and vertices in the figure.'

We note that this relationship is confirmed by all the other
cases we have so far considered. It may be shown that this rule
is general. It is a topological property of the figures we have been
considering, and is known as *Euler's formula*.

There is no need to commit this formula to memory and
schoolchildren should not be made to learn it. The aim of the
exercises given above is merely to sharpen children's interest in
the observation of figures.

Our object is to provide children with an opportunity to
organize their observations systematically, to collect together
the results they have recorded, to note their findings in a clear
and precise form and to work towards the beginnings of experimental verification; in short, to put into practice the pro-
cedures of scientific investigation.

Up to now, all the figures we have studied have been 'all of a piece' (connected). What happens if we consider as one graph two or more disjoint but connected figures, as is the case in Figure 51 (suggested by a nine-year-old pupil)?

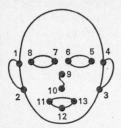

Figure 51

We shall see that the previous formula can easily be generalized. If we do not count the 'infinite' face in which the figures to be studied are embedded, but only faces inside a closed figure, then in Figure 51, for example, six 'faces' may be distinguished: the areas inside the two ears, the two eyes, the mouth and the area inside the face (excluding the eyes and mouth). Then, placing the three terms F, V and E on the left-hand side of the equation we can write

$$F + V - E = n,$$

where n is the number of connected components, that is, the total number of continuous figures in the whole graph. In the example above, n equals five: the connected components are the outline of the human face with the ears attached, the outline of each of the eyes, the outline of the nose and the outline of the mouth. There are thirteen vertices and fourteen edges. We verify that the formula applies:

$$6 + 13 - 14 = 5.$$

We note that if we draw an extra edge between the vertices situated on both eyes, we add one edge and simultaneously reduce by one the number of distinct components so that no new faces are created and the equation remains balanced. We likewise observe that the formula is valid when we are dealing with a figure which is reduced to one point ($V = 1$, $n = 1$).

Finally, what happens when there is no figure at all? This question was raised by a second-form girl who had studied a series of differing figures and was looking for counter-examples. The reader will be able to confirm that the formula still applies.

Exercise. Given the fragment of jigsaw puzzle in Figure 49e, count the number of edges, faces and vertices. Test Euler's formula.

Eulerian circuits

We shall continue to make use of planar topological graphs in the study of what are known as 'Eulerian circuits'.

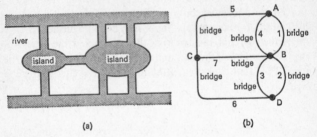

(a)   (b)

Figure 52

The German town of Königsberg (now called Kaliningrad) had paths along the banks of the River Pregel and its two islands which were linked to the banks and to each other by seven bridges, as shown in Figure 52a. It is said that the townsfolk sought in vain for a route which would enable them to make a complete circuit without crossing any bridge twice and without leaving one out. The mathematician Euler studied the problem and demonstrated that it was insoluble.

A problem such as this can usefully be represented as a planar topological graph (Figure 52b). The graph contains four vertices

(A, B, CD,) and seven edges (numbered from one to seven) corresponding to the seven bridges.

Remember that the degree of a vertex is the number of edges which issue from or end at the vertex in question (two in the case of a loop). Euler showed that the parity of this number plays an essential role. Here, A, C and D are of degree three, and B is of degree five; the vertices are all of odd degree.

Now, by way of experiment, let us examine several graphs, enumerating their odd and even vertices and establishing whether or not an Eulerian circuit (that is, one which traverses all the edges without leaving any out and without covering the same one twice) can be found on each graph.

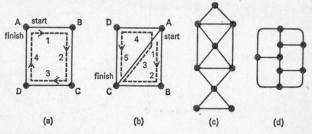

(a)   (b)   (c)   (d)

Figure 53

Consider the various cases represented by the graphs in Figure 53. For graphs (a), (b) and (c) we can readily find an Eulerian circuit (indicated in (a) and (b) by dotted lines). For graph (d) no such circuit can be found:

In (a) all the vertices are of even degree;
In (b) there are two vertices of even degree (B and D) and two vertices of odd degree (A and C);
In (c) all the vertices are of even degree;
In (d) there are eight vertices of odd degree.

We have illustrated the following laws:

1 In any graph, the number of odd vertices is even (thus it is impossible for a graph to have a single odd vertex).

2 The only Eulerian graphs are those in which the number of odd vertices is equal to zero or two. In the first case, the circuit can be started at any point. In the second, the circuit must begin at one of the two odd vertices and terminate at the other. Case (b) falls into this second category.

It was by establishing these rules that Euler was able to state that the problem of the bridges of Königsberg had no solution as, in this case (Figure 52b), all four vertices are odd.

Figure 54a represents the ground floor of a house containing five rooms p, q, r, s, t and sixteen doors numbered one to sixteen, linking the rooms to each other or to the outside u. The next

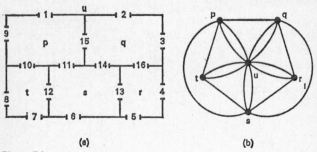

(a)   (b)

Figure 54

exercise consists in finding out whether there exist one or more routes which pass through all the doors once and once only.

The same problem is presented in Figure 54b as a planar topological graph:

1 Verify that this graph is a faithful representation of the situation put forward in the schematic diagram. To what do the edges correspond?

2 By means of the graph show that there is no possible solution to the problem, i.e., there is no Eulerian circuit on the graph.

3 Find which door or doors would have to be eliminated to make the problem soluble.

The topological study of geometric solids

By 'geometric solids' we mean those solids which are related to polyhedra but whose edges are not necessarily straight and whose faces are not necessarily plane. In other words, in studying these solids, we do not take into account the size of the elements of which they are composed, their orientation or the flatness of their surfaces.

The terminology defined in relation to connected planar topological graphs is applicable and the same topics can be discussed as in previous sections, i.e. Euler's formula and the Eulerian circuit.

Euler's formula

Consider the simplest polyhedron, the tetrahedron represented in perspective in Figure 55a. The edge D C, which is not visible, is marked by a dotted line and the face A B C, assumed to be in shadow, is shaded. For this solid we have $F = 4$, $V = 4$ and $E = 6$.

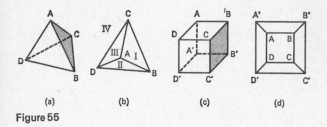

(a)   (b)   (c)   (d)

Figure 55

This tetrahedron may be placed in topological correspondence with the planar graph of Figure 55b, since the vertices and lines pair off with each other (the same capital letters have been used in both cases). We can find four faces on the graph just as we can on the solid figure provided that we count – as we normally do – the connected region outside the lines of the graph as a face. Since Euler's formula is applicable to the graph, it is equally applicable to the tetrahedron.

The same procedure can readily be applied to the case of the cube or the parallelepiped (Figure 55c, 55d). We leave this as an exercise for the reader.

For further exercises, we can in the same way construct more complicated examples of polyhedra – with the help of cardboard or modelling clay – and count the vertices, edges and faces to verify that Euler's formula still holds.

The Eulerian circuit

The principle of the Eulerian circuit on a graph can equally well be transposed to the solids which we are now considering. For instance, we can ask if it is possible to traverse all the edges of the cube in Figure 55c, starting from A, for example, and traversing each edge once only.

The answer is immediately supplied by studying the graph in Figure 55d, which is equivalent to the solid as far as the present problem is concerned. The eight vertices are of odd degree (three) and there is accordingly no solution. We can draw the same conclusion for the tetrahedron, which has four vertices of odd degree.

Chapter 6
From sets of points to 'abstract topological spaces'

In this chapter we propose to give a very brief outline of the extensions to intuitive topology brought about by contemporary mathematics, culminating in topological spaces, which are sets possessing a certain structure and having little or no connection with what is usually called 'space'.

We have already observed that topology developed much more slowly than Euclidean geometry. Apart from Euler, whom we have already mentioned, Descartes (1596–1650) was also a pioneer in this field. But it was not until the nineteenth century and the beginning of the twentieth century that this branch of mathematics took on any importance, with mathematicians such as A. F. Moebius (1790–1868), J. B. Listing (1808–82), B. Riemann (1826–66) and, more recently, Oswald Veblen, Maurice Fréchet, Friedrich Hausdorff, Casimir Kuratowski, Henri Poincaré, Solomon Lefschetz and Nicolas Bourbaki (a pseudonym adopted by a 'collective' of mathematicians which is continually being renewed).

During its first years of existence, the discipline (known by the name of *analysis situs*) was permeated with classical geometry and reasoning was carried out on the basis of geometric configurations. It is to this kind of topology that we have confined ourselves in the present work.

Subsequently, as part of the revolution which brought about the unification of the various branches of mathematics under the heading of 'set theory', topology, in adopting a similar viewpoint, became concerned with 'topological spaces' defined abstractly from axioms which have no intuitive connection with space.

There is no question of presenting here a rigorous exposition of this formal topology. We simply wish to indicate to the reader by means of a few illustrations, presented naïvely in order to make them more accessible, the way in which formal mathematics – the only true mathematics – deals with the problems which fall within its domain.

We begin with a set T of 'mathematical entities' not otherwise defined. We distinguish within this set certain subsets f which include the set T itself and the null set $\emptyset$.

Considered together, these subsets constitute a system $\{F\}$ and if:

(a) The union of any number of members of $\{F\}$ is a member of $\{F\}$,

(b) The intersection of any two members of $\{F\}$ is a member of $\{F\}$,

then the pair $[T, \{F\}]$ is called a topological space.

Let us illustrate this definition with some examples.

Examples

1 Consider a set T of four objects (Figure 56a),

$$T = \{\triangledown, \ominus, \bigcirc, \square\}.$$

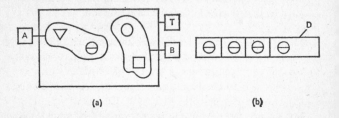

(a)   (b)

Let A be the subset $\{\triangledown, \ominus\}$ and B be the subset $\{\bigcirc, \square\}$.
Consider the system $\{F\}$,

$$\{F\} = \{\emptyset\, A, B, T\}.$$

The rules of composition of the members of $\{F\}$ for the operations of union ($\cup$) and intersection ($\cap$) allow us to state that the conditions (a) and (b) which are necessary conditions for a topological space are satisfied. For example,

$A \cap B = \emptyset,$
$A \cup B = T.$

The set T together with the system $\{F\}$ constitutes a topological space. The members of the system $\{F\}$ are called the 'open sets' of the space. In particular, the empty set is an open set, as also is the set T itself.

2 Let there be a set T of n elements $a, b, c, \ldots, n$,

$T = \{a, b, c, \ldots, n\}.$

Let us define $\mathcal{P}(T)$ to be the system of all the partitions of T. Then T together with $\mathcal{P}(T)$ is a topological space; all the partitions of T, for example $\{a, b, c\}$, $\{b, c, d, n\}$, are its open sets. 3 This is another way of looking at the previous example and is intended to indicate the connection between the topological spaces which we have just defined and sets of geometric points.

Consider a finite set D of dominoes each bearing an identifying number (Figure 56) and also the system $\{L\}$ of subsets which we can form by taking successively no dominoes, one domino, ..., all the dominoes. According to what we have just seen, D together with $\{L\}$ constitutes a topological space.

Let us now assume that we use increasingly small and numerous dominoes. When placed end to end they will form a continuous line from the first to the last domino. This group of 'domino-points' and the system of subsets associated with it appears as a generalization of the previous discrete spaces. It makes the connection between spaces which have no reference to spatial data and those which were invented in order to represent spatial configurations.

Let us return to our original definition in order to make the terminology more precise, following Bourbaki (1964) and Patterson (1959).

The set T with which we begin is a set of mathematical entities called *points*. The system $\{F\}$ of open sets defines on T a topological structure (or *topology*) for T. Thus a topological space is a set of points together with a topology.

From what has gone before, we see that 'a set together with a topological structure' means that there are interconnections of certain elements of the set, which follow certain rules. In the first example, element ∇ and element $\ominus$ have been linked, on the one hand and elements $\bigcirc$ and $\square$ on the other. However, ∇ and $\bigcirc$ have not been linked as this would have formed a bridge between the two original linkings.

Intuitively there is a spatial element underlying these linkings in the same way that such an element is implicit in the operations of union and intersection to which the definition of topological structure refers.

But there is no such element in the axiomatic world of the mathematician. He is disengaged from all reference to sensory experience; he retains only a kind of 'shadow' whose origin in the real world is uncertain. The freedom gained through this ability of abstraction is paid for by a loss in terms of representability. The developments of the study of formal topological spaces do not lend themselves to representation, since all representation is revealed as inadequate, which explains why the works on formal topology, in contrast to those on Euclidean geometry, resort only rarely to illustrations, sometimes not doing so at all.

This being so, the study of topological spaces develops according to a procedure parallel to that followed in the topological study of configurations of points, whose general architecture we have previously summarized.

This study introduces the concepts of neighbourhood which was defined by Bourbaki (1964, p. 3): 'In a topological space T, we describe as a *neighbourhood* of a subset A of T, any set which contains an open set containing A'. Thus in example 1, the set $V = \{\nabla, \square, \bigcirc\}$ contains the set $A = \{\nabla, \square\}$ which is an open set; V is therefore a neighbourhood of A. It also introduces the concepts of *interior* and *exterior*, of *boundary* and *connectivity*, and of *homeomorphism*. This last term designates a bijective mapping between two topological spaces T and T' which conserves their respective topological properties and, in particular, establishes correspondence between the open set of T and the open set T', and conversely.

In the course of this study, we are led to examine in particular the metrisable topological spaces for which we can define a *distance*. In this case, the previous concepts take on a more concrete aspect, for a neighbourhood of a point now appears as the set of points which surround it and are close to it.

The real number line, a set of geometric points provided with the structure of a topological space by considering the system of all linkings of points (or intervals), appears as the prototype of the metrisable topological structure. The circle provides another representative example in which the arcs of the circle play the same role as that of the intervals on the real line.

We thus return, after a long diversion, to familiar ground, perhaps deriving some benefit from the presence of these concepts even if they have not been fully understood.

Conclusion

As the reader has been working his way through these pages, he has – or so we hope – been able to build up an increasingly clear picture of the concepts covered by the very general vocabulary of topology. Similarly, we hope that we have persuaded him to share our conviction of the importance of topological concepts, for both children and adults, at the levels of general education and of everyday life.

Referring very briefly to the work of the Bourbaki team, it emerges that the totality of concepts studied by mathematics reduces to three fundamental structures, which Bourbaki calls 'mother structures'.
These are:

'Algebraic structures', whose prototype is the group;
'Order structures', which are concerned with relationships, and of which the most significant example is the network (lattice);
'Topological structures', which are based on the concepts of neighbourhood, continuity and limit.

In doing this, the Bourbaki group reached a conclusion extremely close to that arrived at by the psychologist Piaget, following a completely different route. He recalls the astonishment of both the mathematician Dieudonné and himself, when, on meeting in Melun in 1952 at a conference on mathematical and mental structures, they realized that their respective points of view coincided closely, although they had never previously had the opportunity of comparing their work (Piaget and Beth 1961). A convergence such as this is indeed remarkable and can only support our conviction of the fundamental nature of topology.

In progressing through this work, however, the reader will undoubtedly have observed another characteristic. At the level at which we have been considering it, topology constantly returns to what can be described as a visual language. Planar graphs are diagrams which speak for themselves. They make use of a visual vocabulary which is very simple since it is composed entirely of vertices, boundaries and regions and a syntax which possesses only a minimal number of rules.

This language, in spite of its impoverishment, is nevertheless capable of expressing complex relational situations which may apparently have nothing in common with specifically spatial problems.

The use of this language is advantageous in many situations. It is particularly easy to memorize and it allows for interactions between the processes of analysis and synthesis: when we study a diagram we can use it to detail each part in turn, carrying out an analytical process, or to characterize the complete figure, carrying out a process of synthesis.

In this work, we have tried to provide several examples of the use of this language, since we are convinced that it is going to play an increasingly important role in our technological world. The ability to read at a glance the graph which describes in simplified form the maze of a motorway interchange, the ability to understand the mine of information provided by the schematic wiring diagram of a piece of electronic equipment, the ability to decode the flow diagram for a project – these are eminently useful areas of knowledge.

We can only hope that the reader who has placed his faith in us and followed us over the difficult terrain into which we have sometimes led him will not regret the effort but will find himself better equipped to understand not only the situations illustrated by our particular examples, but also some of the great structures which the science of today puts at the disposal of man as the universal instruments of knowledge.

References

BOURBAKI, N. (1964), *Topologie générale, fascicule de résultats*, Hermann, Paris.

GARDNER, M. (1967), 'Mathematical games', *Scientific American*, vol. 217, no. 1.

GARDNER, M. (1970), 'Mathematical games', *Scientific American*, vol. 223, no. 4.

LAURENDEAU, M., and PINARD, A. (1968), *Les premières notions spatiales de l'enfant*, Delachaux & Niestlé.

PATTERSON, E. M. (1959), *Topology*, Oliver & Boyd.

PIAGET, J. (1954), *Construction of Reality in the Child*, Routledge & Kegan Paul.

PIAGET, J., and BETH, E. (1951), *Épistémologie mathématique et psychologie*, Presses Universitaires de France.

PIAGET, J., and INHELDER, B. (1956), *The Child's Conception of Space*, Routledge & Kegan Paul.

PIAGET, J., INHELDER, B., and SZEMINSKA, A. (1960), *The Child's Conception of Geometry*, Routledge & Kegan Paul.

REVUZ, A., and REVUZ, G. (1966), *Le cours de l'A.P.M. III, elements de topologie*, APMEP, Paris.

WALLON, H. (1945), *Les origines de la pensée chez l'enfant*.

Further Reading

I. ADLER, *The New Mathematics*, Dobson, 1964.

C. BERGE, *Topological Spaces*, Oliver & Boyd, 1963.

R. COURANT and H. ROBBINS, *What is Mathematics?*, Oxford University Press, 1969.

Z. P. DIENES, *Exploration of Space and Practical Measurement*, Educational Supply Association, 1969.

T. J. FLETCHER (ed.), *Some Lessons in Mathematics*, Cambridge University Press, 1964.

P. R. HALMOS, *Naive Set Theory*, Van Nostrand, 1960.

O. ORE, *Graphs and Their Uses*, Random House, 1963.

E. M. PATTERSON, *Topology*, Oliver & Boyd, 1959.